Epic
Voyages

Epic Voyages

Hawys Morgan

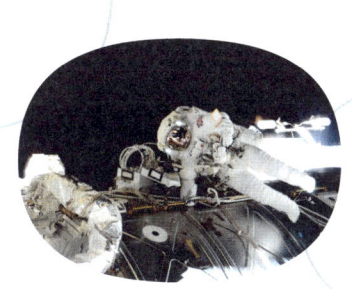

Collins

Contents

Bonus: Explorers' map 2

1 Viking voyager 4

Bonus: A Viking longship 16

2 Insect hunter 18

Bonus: Silk moths 30

3 Secret sailor 32

Bonus: Jeanne's route around the world 44

4 Magnificent map-maker 46

Bonus: Supplies for racing to the North 58

5 Deep-sea diver 60

Bonus: Our oceans 70

6 Star tracker 72

Bonus: The International Space Station 82

Glossary 84

About the author 86

About the illustrator 88

Book chat 90

Bonus
Explorers' map

NORTH AMERICA

Atlantic Ocean

Pacific Ocean

SOUTH AMERICA

1 Viking voyager

Leif Erikson (approx. 970–1020)

More than a thousand years ago, a Viking longship sailed all the way to the east coast of North America. The captain was Leif Erikson, also known as 'Leif the Lucky'. He and his crew became the first Europeans to set foot in North America. How do you think he might have felt?

Well, Leif hadn't planned to land in North America, so he probably felt confused and a little worried!

Leif had been sailing to Greenland when a storm blew his ship off course. Leif and his crew landed in North America by accident!

The Vikings were originally from Scandinavia – the area that is now Sweden, Denmark and Norway. So how did Leif end up so far away from his Viking homeland?

Leif's father was a Viking explorer called Erik the Red. This name was perfect because Erik had red hair and a red-hot temper!

Your Viking name

The Vikings liked descriptive names for people and places. Make your own Viking name!

Your first name + the + a word that describes you, for example:

Olivia the Goal-scorer

Rayan the Chatty

Yusuf the Artist

Originally, Erik the Red lived in Scandinavia. However, Erik and his family kept getting into arguments and fights. Eventually, they had annoyed so many people that they had to leave. They moved to Iceland where Leif was born, but things didn't go much better in Iceland.

Erik the Red's short temper got the better of him again. He argued violently with neighbours and as punishment, he had to leave Iceland.

The family travelled west across the sea until eventually they settled in Greenland. Life would have been hard for Erik, Leif and the rest of the family. Few people lived there, so there was no one to buy food or other supplies from. If you wanted to eat, you had to find food for yourself, by hunting, fishing and farming.

Erik the Red named the island Greenland because when he first arrived it was summer, and the land was covered in green meadows. However, for much of the year, Greenland is a cold and icy place and it's not green at all! Farming was tough work. The soil was often frozen hard and in winter there was very little sunlight.

Erik hoped the name Greenland would encourage other Vikings to settle there, too.

Leif's mistake: The wrong way home

When Leif grew up, he left Greenland and travelled back to Scandinavia to work for a Viking king. After a few years, it was time for Leif to return to Greenland to his family. He made the long, dangerous journey across the Atlantic Ocean in his longship. A huge storm dragged the ship off course. When the storm cleared, the crew spied the shores of North America ahead of them.

Leif and his crew had already spent a long time at sea, sleeping on the deck of the ship. Their supplies were beginning to run out. They must have been relieved to see land, even if it wasn't the land they were expecting to see!

The first part of the North American coastline they came to was flat, and covered in rocks and ice. This didn't seem like a great place to set up camp, so Leif and his crew sailed further south.

As Leif travelled down the coast, he named the new places he saw. Leif named places in a very literal way, describing what he saw. This was because the Vikings did not use paper maps. Descriptive names like 'Land of Flat Rocks' would help the Vikings easily identify where they were. This was helpful if they wanted to remember a journey, or if they wanted to give other Vikings directions.

Naming these places would help Leif find this coastline again in the future if he wanted to.

These are some of the names Leif gave to places in North America and what they mean:

Helluland – Land of Flat Rocks

Markland – Land of Forests

Vinland – Land of **Vines**

From these names, we know Leif used landmarks such as rocks and forests to find his way. Leif probably used other Viking ways of **navigating** without maps, too.

How could Leif navigate?

- The sun – it always rises in the east and sets in the west so watching the sun helped him work out in which direction he was travelling.
- Star-watching – the North Star showed where north was at night.
- Watching animals – certain birds, such as puffins, are only seen near land so Leif would know he was near shore if he saw one. Whales follow specific routes across the oceans so if he wanted to go the same way, he could follow the whales. In fact, the Vikings called the sea the 'whale-road'.

Leif and his crew continued down the coast past an area covered in thick forests. Further south they found an island. There were plenty of fish, the land was good for growing plants and there was wood for building houses and ships. It was an ideal spot to rest and build up their supplies.

Leif and his crew set up camp in this spot. Experts believe the area Leif settled in is the eastern coast of modern-day Canada.

They met the Native American people who had always lived in this area of North America. To begin with, Leif and his crew lived peacefully side by side with the Native American people. They **traded** food and other items.

But before long, the Vikings and the Native American people started fighting each other. Eventually, Leif and the other Vikings decided it was too risky to stay there and they returned north to Greenland.

It would take another 500 years for European explorers to reach North America once more.

Bonus

A Viking longship

The Vikings were expert shipbuilders and navigators. Viking longships were sturdy and coped well with stormy seas.

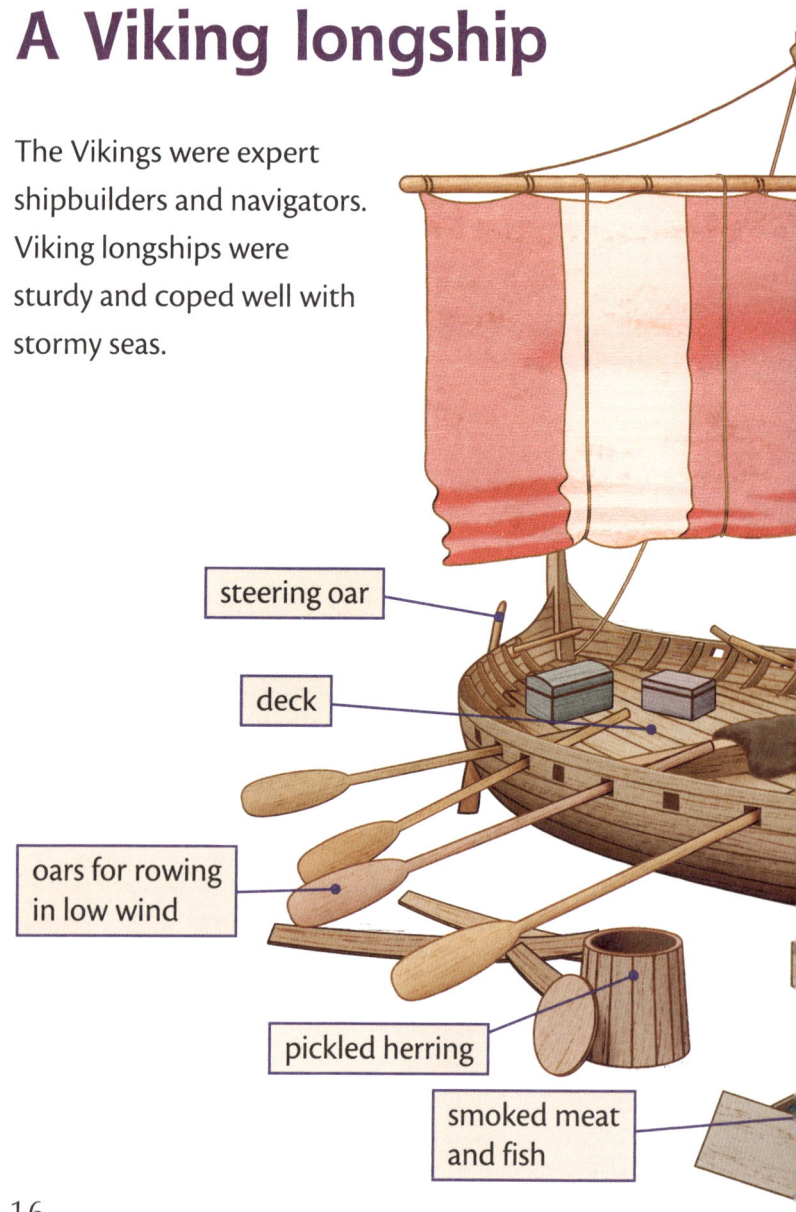

- steering oar
- deck
- oars for rowing in low wind
- pickled herring
- smoked meat and fish

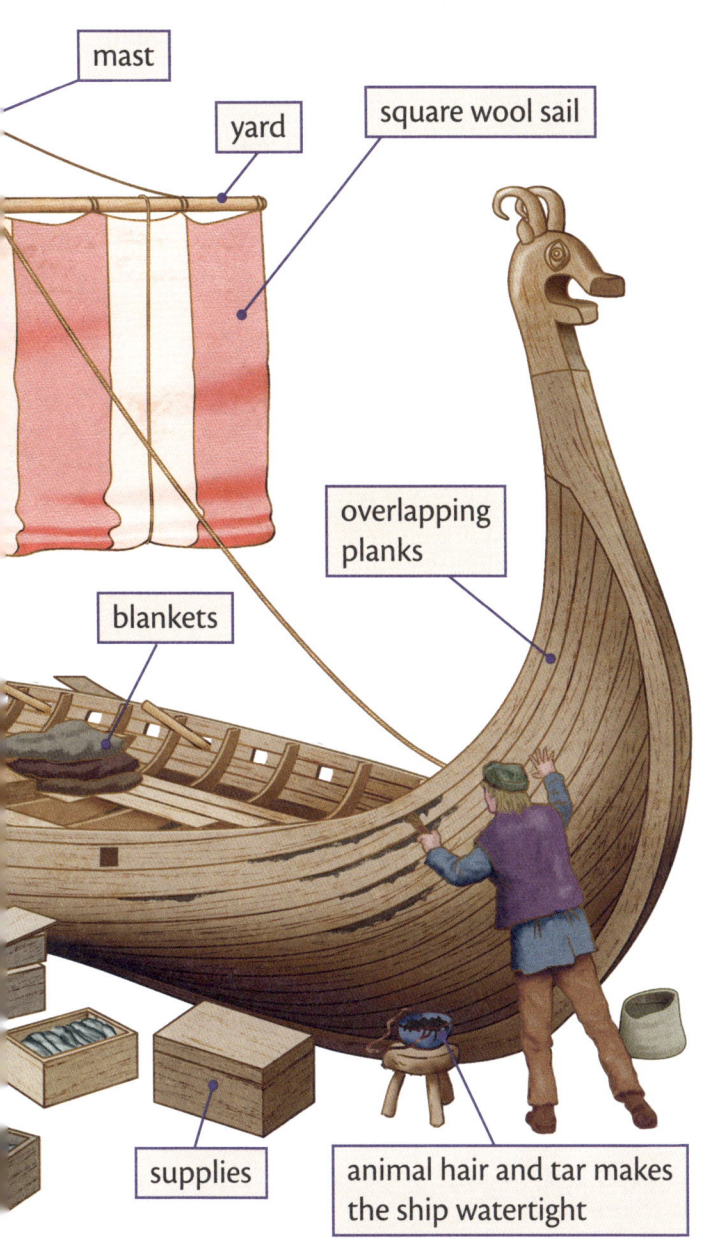

2 Insect hunter

Maria Sibylla Merian (1647–1717)

Maria Sybilla Merian was born in Germany over 300 years ago. Her voyage of discovery took her across the Atlantic Ocean to the jungles of South America. She did this at a time when women rarely travelled long distances.

Maria's family were all artists. They ran a business making books about Central and South America with beautiful pictures. She grew up surrounded by their pictures and books and she dreamed of seeing Central and South America herself.

Maria's stepfather was an artist who specialised in painting flowers. Maria had lessons from him and she was soon learning to be an artist herself. She painted realistic pictures of not only plants and flowers, but also the insects that lived on or near them.

At that time, women and girls often didn't go to school and they weren't taught about science. However, Maria was obsessed with insects. She found silkworm caterpillars especially interesting. She wanted to know more about them, even if she couldn't go to school.

silkworm

At the time, people didn't know much about the life cycle of insects. Many people believed they magically came from dust, mud or rotten meat.

Maria wasn't convinced by these ideas. She wanted to know what really happened. As a child, she collected and kept insects. She observed them every day. She made notes and drawings of what they did, what they ate and how they changed over time.

By the time she was 13, Maria had worked out the life cycle of a silkworm caterpillar!

Unfortunately, she didn't have a way of sharing this knowledge with other people. At that time very few women, let alone 13-year-old girls, wrote science books. That was because women weren't usually allowed to learn about science at school or university.

In 1665, Maria got married and later had two daughters, Dorothea and Johanna. She spent the next 14 years painting realistic pictures of flowers and publishing them in books. The first books she published weren't science books. They simply contained pictures of flowers.

While painting flowers, she observed which insects lived on the plants or ate them. Maria included insects in almost every flower picture she painted. Her curiosity about insects, and in particular caterpillars, grew and grew.

In 1679, she finally published her book on caterpillars. This was 19 years after she first discovered the life cycle of a silkworm caterpillar. She was one of the first people to describe in detail the life cycle of a butterfly.

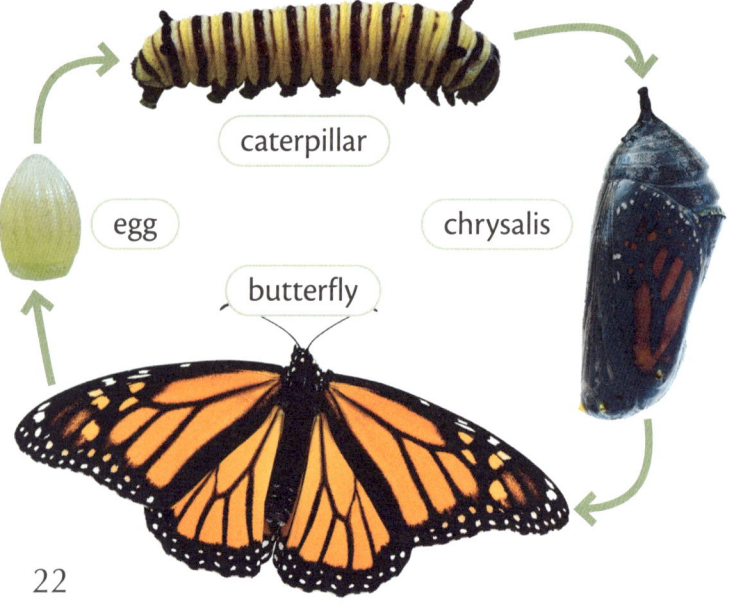

Scientists across Europe were impressed by how accurate her caterpillar book was. Maria gained a reputation as a serious scientific painter and **naturalist.**

In 1691, Maria got divorced. She and her daughters moved to Amsterdam, an important city in the Netherlands. She visited museums and met scientists who showed her collections of insects and plants collected from Central and South America.

She examined these collections and imagined huge bright blue butterflies flying around fiery red flowers in hot jungles.

She was fascinated by the insects and was determined to see them alive in their natural habitat, rather than in dusty glass boxes. Maria decided to go to Suriname, a small country on the northern coast of South America. Travelling across the Atlantic Ocean was not easy at the time, especially for women. Men and women weren't treated equally. Women usually couldn't travel without a male family member, such as a husband, father or brother.

In the 1690s, Suriname was ruled by the Dutch. There were no planes or trains in those days, so the only way to travel to Suriname was by ship.

Maria sold most of her belongings and many paintings to raise enough money for her trip. Her plan was to do research into plants and animals in the jungle. Maria risked everything to go on this adventure.

In 1699, at the age of 52, Maria left Europe with her now grown-up daughter Dorothea. They had an uncomfortable and dangerous voyage across the ocean. It took two months to reach Suriname, but it was worth it. Maria had dreamed of making a journey like this since she was a little girl. Now she was finally here.

Maria and her daughter made many trips into the countryside. Local guides hacked paths through the thick plants and trees so Maria could explore deep into the jungle.

They often had to fight their way through clouds of biting black flies, but that didn't put Maria off.

These jungles were teeming with fascinating insects. Maria and Dorothea spent hours observing and painting new species of plants and animals. They wrote detailed notes about the colourful butterflies, huge spiders and hungry caterpillars they saw there.

These trips into the **humid** jungle were hard work in the heavy, long skirts women were expected to wear back then.

Sadly, after just two years, Maria had to leave Suriname because she was very ill.

She returned to Amsterdam with her drawings and samples of dried insects and plants.

She spent the next few years turning her research into a ground-breaking book about nature in Suriname. It was very popular because it was beautiful and it explained new scientific ideas about nature. She showed the link between insects and the plants they chose to live near and eat.

Maria refused to be limited by what society thought women should or shouldn't do.

She taught her daughters, Dorothea and Johanna, to draw and paint. They followed in her footsteps, becoming respected artists themselves. Dorothea even ended up moving to Suriname!

Maria was greatly respected by other scientists. Even today, naturalists like Sir David Attenborough believe that Maria made a huge contribution to the study of insects and plants.

Things named in Maria's honour

9 butterflies
6 plants
2 insects
A spider
A lizard

Bonus

Silk moths

Silk moth caterpillars can make strands of silk nearly a kilometre long! Several strands are twisted together to make silk thread. This thread is then used to make silk cloth. Clothes made from silk cloth are very soft and warm.

After a week or two, the eggs hatch into caterpillars.

A silk moth lays about 400 eggs on a mulberry plant.

The caterpillars eat the mulberry leaves and grow.

Each caterpillar makes a **cocoon** out of one single strand of silk.

A new silk moth comes out of the cocoon.

3 Secret sailor

Jeanne Baret (1740–1807)

Jeanne Baret was born in France in 1740. Men and women were not treated equally at this time. It was still frowned upon for women to travel much, let alone become explorers.

Jeanne was special because she didn't just travel across one ocean – she was the first woman to **circumnavigate** the globe!

Jeanne grew up in the countryside. Her family were poor farmers. Like many girls back then, Jeanne never had the chance to go to school.

When she was little, she spent as much time as possible outside. She was fascinated by plants. As she got older, she learned about how they can be used to treat common illnesses. Friends and neighbours often came to her for advice when they were unwell.

When Jeanne was a young woman, a wealthy man called Philibert Commerson moved into the area. Like Jeanne, Philibert studied plants and their uses. Philibert gave Jeanne a job taking care of his house.

Jeanne and Philibert liked sharing what they knew about plants with each other. They soon became good friends.

In 1765, a ship's captain in the French navy asked Philibert to join him on an exciting voyage around the globe. The French captain wanted Philibert to record all the new plants they discovered on their voyage. Philibert wanted Jeanne to come as his assistant, but women were forbidden to board French navy ships. This rule wasn't going to stop Jeanne and Philibert.

Jeanne shortened her name to the boy's name 'Jean' and disguised herself as a man. She managed to trick the captain into believing she was a young man. She was allowed to board his ship, *'The Star'*.

Below decks, most of the crew lived together in cramped conditions with no private spaces. Luckily, Philibert and Jeanne had their own cabin.

The first part of Jeanne's journey was across the Atlantic Ocean. To begin with, Philibert and Jeanne collected plants together, but Philibert soon became unwell.

Philibert felt weak and spent most of his time in their cabin. He had to leave Jeanne to do most of the work.

The ship sailed south to Brazil where Jeanne saw plants no European person had seen before. The landscape changed as they moved down into southern Argentina. The humid jungles of central America were gone.

The weather got colder as they travelled south. Soon they were sailing past icebergs and groups of penguins and seals.

The ship passed through a channel linking the Atlantic Ocean and the Pacific Ocean and moved up the west coast of South America.

For over a year, Jeanne successfully tricked the crew of 100 men into believing she was a man. Afraid of what would happen if they discovered the truth, she kept herself to herself. Philibert was still sick, so she spent a lot of her time looking after him in their cabin.

In 1767, about half-way between South America and Australia, the ship docked on the beautiful island of Tahiti. Jeanne went ashore to research the plants on the island. The people living there quickly realised she was in fact a woman. They threatened to reveal her secret.

Back on the ship that afternoon, Jeanne decided it was safer to tell the crew her secret. They were furious that she had fooled them. Life became difficult and dangerous for Jeanne. The ship stayed anchored in Tahiti for months. Jeanne was thousands of miles from home, and surrounded by men who didn't want her on the ship.

No other ships were likely to arrive in Tahiti any time soon. If Jeanne and Philibert didn't leave on *The Star*, they might be stranded on the island. The crew reluctantly agreed they could stay on the ship for now.

Poor Jeanne was rarely allowed to leave the cabin. It must have been stressful and lonely for her.

They sailed north of Australia into the Indian Ocean, but then things took a turn for the worse. The wind dropped and the ship moved slowly across the still waters.

Sickness spread around the ship. The crew started to run out of food and water and they had to eat the ship's rats. The excitement of adventure and discovery had vanished. All that mattered now was survival.

Finally, the ship arrived in Jakarta, a port in Indonesia, where the crew could restock.

The Star sailed on towards the east coast of Africa. Jeanne had had enough of being stuck in her cabin for days on end and Philibert was still sick. She and Philibert decided to leave the ship when it docked at the island of Mauritius in 1768.

They stayed in Mauritius for several years, collecting and recording more than 1,000 species of plants. Philibert was still very unwell and Jeanne looked after him until he died in 1773.

After Philibert's death, Jeanne had to look after herself. She worked in a café where she met a French soldier. They got married and decided to return to France. Thankfully, this time Jeanne didn't have to pretend to be a man. By returning to France, she became the first woman to circumnavigate the globe, 10 years after she left!

In that time, she saw jungles, **glaciers**, deserts and other landscapes her teenage self could never have imagined.

During Jeanne's travels, she collected more than 6,000 valuable plant samples. Sadly, she wasn't given the credit for this collection at the time. Philibert got the credit, even though he had been too unwell during the voyage to collect many plants.

However, ten years after she returned to France, the French navy recognised her courage and scientific research.

In 2012, a plant was named after Jeanne, and in 2018 a chain of mountains on the dwarf planet, Pluto, was named after this brave explorer.

Bonus
Jeanne's route around the world

4 Magnificent map-maker

Matthew Henson (1866–1955)

Matthew Henson's travels took him to the top of the world. He was one of the first people to set foot on the North Pole.

Matthew's parents were poor farmers in the United States. Sadly, they both died when he was a young boy. For the next eight years, Matthew lived with his uncle. He left school when he was just 12 and started looking for work.

Matthew loved stories about the sea, so he was excited when a ship's captain offered him a job. The captain taught Matthew how to read, write and be a good sailor. For six happy years they travelled far and wide together.

Tragedy struck again, though, when the captain became unwell at sea and died. Matthew didn't want to stay on the ship without the kind captain, so he left the ship and found a job in a hat shop.

When Matthew was 22, he met an explorer called Robert Peary in the shop. Robert was planning a trip to Central America. They started chatting about Matthew's years at sea. Robert liked Matthew, so he offered him a job as his assistant on his next voyage. Matthew couldn't wait to return to the sea.

Their first trip was to Central America where they made maps of the jungle. For two years they explored the humid jungles and became close friends.

That was their last trip to a hot country. Their future voyages would all be to the frozen far north.

Together they made many difficult and dangerous voyages to the Arctic. On one trip they sledged over 2,100 km to north-eastern Greenland to prove it was an island. They made detailed maps of the whole of the Greenland ice cap. These maps would prove very useful in future visits to the Arctic.

Robert couldn't ask for a better teammate by his side.

Matthew learned to speak the **Inuit** language and was welcomed by the local Inuit people. They called him 'Matthew the Kind One'.

Matthew learned new skills quickly. He was good at learning languages, fixing things, fishing and dog-sledding. Matthew's Inuit friends taught him about the land, the weather, hunting and how best to travel across the Arctic. They even taught him how to make **igloos** out of snow so Matthew and Robert would have shelter out on the ice.

In the 1890s, explorers from across the world were competing to be the first to reach the North Pole. Robert and Matthew wanted to get there before anyone else.

It was a difficult challenge because you had to do most of the journey either on foot or by dog-sled. The weather could change without warning. One minute it would be sunny and calm, the next there would be a terrible snowstorm. If it was too warm, the ice underfoot might melt and crack.

Robert and Matthew made their first unsuccessful attempt to reach the North Pole in 1893.

After researching different routes to the North Pole, they tried again in 1905. First, they travelled by ship, and then they swapped to sledges. But, the weather was bad for sledging, so they had to abandon this second attempt.

Matthew and Robert didn't give up. In 1908, they set off for the North Pole a third and final time.

22 men, 19 sledges and 113 dogs travelled for months across the freezing ice. Matthew's skills as a carpenter, dog-sledder, hunter and fisherman helped them survive.

There were many scary moments, including the ice cracking open in front of them. There was a real risk of a sledge falling through a crack into the deadly cold waters. The team was cold, hungry and tired. One by one, members of the group gave up and turned back, but not Matthew and Robert.

Only Matthew, Robert and four Inuit hunters remained from the original group.

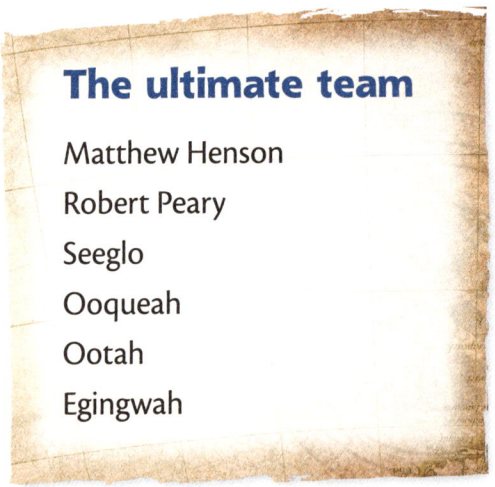

The ultimate team

Matthew Henson
Robert Peary
Seeglo
Ooqueah
Ootah
Egingwah

They raced across the icy wilderness on five dog sledges, travelling for up to 14 hours at a time. They were worried that one of the large cracks in the ice would get bigger, blocking their route back to safety. Most of the time, Matthew travelled slightly ahead, finding the best route across the ice.

Other explorers were trying to reach the North Pole too. The race was on to get there first. And Matthew's team was determined to win

History was made on 6th April, 1909.

The explorers were camping out in igloos on the ice. They woke up to find the sun blocked by thick mist. Travel was impossible because of the weather. The next day, the mist cleared and they checked their position. The North Pole was just behind their igloos! Finally, after travelling 270 kilometres across ice and snow, they had reached the North Pole.

The group checked their footprints in the snow. They discovered that the first person to reach the exact point of the North Pole had been Matthew Henson the day before in the mist. Matthew couldn't believe it!

After all these years of trying to reach the North Pole, he was the first person to do it. His childhood in the countryside and his years selling hats must have felt like a distant memory to him at that moment.

On their return, Robert took all the glory. People of colour were not treated equally, so Matthew and the four Inuit hunters were sadly ignored.

In 1944, Matthew finally received a medal from the American government. Then in 1954, he received an award from the President of the USA himself. He died a year later.

Matthew described his fascination with the Arctic:

"The lure of the Arctic is tugging at my heart."

Bonus

Supplies for racing to the North Pole

Arctic explorers took four basic food supplies with them when they were sledging across the ice. These were foods that would give the explorers energy, and they didn't weigh much. They were:

- tea

- tinned pemmican – a survival food made from fat, dried meat and dried fruit

- ship's biscuits – long-lasting, hard savoury biscuits

- tinned condensed milk – sweet, thick milk.

husky dogs

5 Deep-sea diver

Jill Heinerth (1965–)

Jill Heinerth is an expert deep-sea diver and underwater explorer. She is also a writer, photographer and film-maker. Her books, photos, TV shows and films describe the incredible places she has explored.

Hidden beneath the waves across the world's oceans, there are vast **networks** of caves. Jill specialises in diving down to these underwater caves. She makes maps and takes photos and videos of the caves. Jill has dived with polar bears in Canada and avoided alligators in the Florida swamps.

Jill was born in Canada in 1965. From a young age, she loved swimming in lakes and exploring the natural world. That sense of adventure she had as a young girl still takes her on exciting journeys of discovery in our planet's oceans.

As a young woman, Jill worked as an artist. However, she decided that a life working indoors was not for her. She left Canada and moved to the Caribbean. There, she spent her days diving, writing and taking underwater photos. She became well known as an expert diver and she has had some incredible diving experiences.

On a trip to an island called Lanzarote, Jill and the scientists she was working with discovered a new species. It was a worm smaller than a grain of rice! It has no eyes and is see-through.

One time off the coast of Canada, Jill and her team encountered a group of a hundred humpback whales. Another time, a huge sea lion pulled her up to the sea's surface by tugging at the hood of her diving suit. Not all the animals she has encountered have been friendly. She was once bitten by a poisonous water snake!

We usually think of caves as spaces carved out of rock. However, under the freezing seawater of the Antarctic, there are networks of caves made of a very different material – ice! Jill was the first explorer to create maps of this network of ice caves. She was also one of the first people to ever dive inside an iceberg. Can you imagine what that might have been like?

Jill and her team created a 3D map of this icy underwater landscape. She even swam for more than 3 km into an iceberg cave. This was a record-breaking distance, made even more impressive because the water Jill was swimming through was so cold.

Cave diving can be very dangerous. Not only are many caves extremely long and narrow, the deepest underwater caves are also pitch-black. There can be dangerous obstacles that are tricky to spot with just a diving torch or light. Jill often has to squeeze through tiny spaces, and sometimes the only way to the surface is to go back the way she came.

Divers also have a limited amount of air in their diving tanks, so Jill can't stay underwater for too long.

One time, Jill and her co-divers were trapped in an iceberg cave for nearly two hours. Eventually, they managed to escape, but it was a close call.

For these reasons, Jill needs to be very organised. She must plan carefully where she will explore, what equipment she will need and how long she can stay underwater.

Jill says that it is natural to feel afraid before a dive, but it is important to control that fear. Panicking can cause mistakes. However, there's an even more serious danger if a diver lets the fear take over. Fear can make you breathe more quickly. This uses up more air, and underwater, air is in short supply. Jill has learned to keep calm and form a plan when faced with danger.

When planning for a deep dive, Jill has to be aware of any risks. These could include:

- Obstacles like rocks that might damage equipment or cause an injury.
- Narrow routes through caves or shipwrecks where she might get stuck.
- Dangerous animals, such as poisonous jellyfish or water snakes.
- Water that is too warm or too cold.
- **Currents** that might pull her off course, or stop her from moving forward.

So why does Jill risk going to these dangerous depths? Jill loves discovering places that no one has visited before. More people have been to the moon than to some of the caves Jill has explored beneath the surface of our planet. She also wants to help other people understand how precious this underwater world is.

Jill has another mission: to find freshwater. She thinks there may be freshwater hidden underneath the earth. Freshwater is vital for us all as this is the water we drink and we cannot survive without it. We can look after the planet's freshwater by reducing how much water we use and preventing water pollution.

Jill also wants to raise awareness of **climate change**. The Arctic is warming faster than any other place on our planet. On her diving trips to the Arctic, Jill can measure how and where the sea ice is melting.

Melting sea ice makes the sea level rise across the world. Scientists think this will cause flooding in some places.

It also causes problems for many animals that live in the Arctic, such as polar bears. In the past, polar bears would hunt seals on the ice. Less ice means the polar bears have to swim longer distances to search for food. This makes them tired and less able to hunt successfully.

Jill has won many awards for her diving and climate work, including the Canada Polar Medal and Sea Hero of the Year. She has over 7,000 dives under her belt and she's still counting! Thanks to Jill, we now know much more about the hidden world of underwater caves and the secrets they hold. Who knows what she will discover next in our deep oceans?

Bonus
Our oceans

Our oceans make up almost all of Earth's water. This water is saltwater.

Atlantic Ocean

Pacific Ocean

Only about a quarter of the seafloor has been mapped.

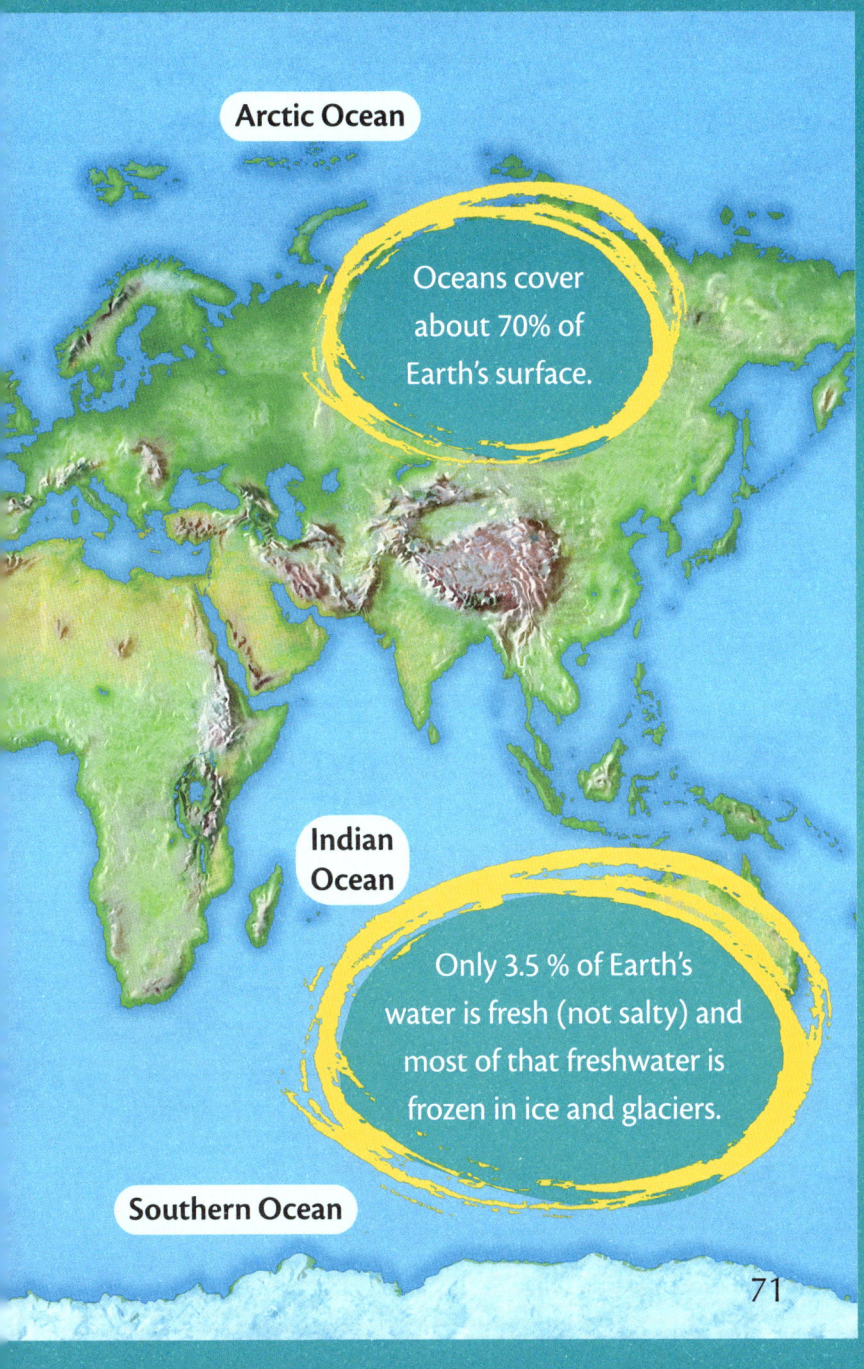

6 Star tracker

Tim Peake (1972–)

As a boy, Tim Peake liked to imagine what it would be like to fly high above the clouds. Little did he know that one day he would travel far beyond those clouds, into space!

Tim was born in the United Kingdom. He loved adventure and was happiest being outdoors. His favourite hobbies were hiking, kayaking and climbing. Tim and his father enjoyed watching air shows together, where different types of aircraft performed exciting stunts and demonstrations. Tim's fascination with flying grew from there.

When Tim was 13, he learned to fly planes at an after-school club. By the time he was 18, he had flown planes by himself several times.

After finishing school, Tim joined the British Army. There, he learned how to fly helicopters. His job took him all over the world. Tim loved his work and he was good at it.

Tim had never really thought about being an astronaut. Then in 2009, he saw an advert for the European Space Agency. They were looking for new astronauts! Tim wanted a new challenge so he applied. The competition was fierce and over 8,000 people applied. After a year of challenging tests, the European Space Agency chose Tim and five of his classmates to go to the International Space Station.

The International Space Station is a large spacecraft that travels around Earth. It travels super-fast. It takes just 92 minutes to go all the way around the Earth. This means that astronauts on the space station can see 16 sunrises and sunsets every day!

Astronauts live on the space station, do science experiments on board and learn about the universe. Several different countries built the space station together, and now astronauts from across the world share it. Teamwork is essential on the Space Station. Over several years, Tim and his teammates trained together in the United States, Russia, Japan, Canada and Germany.

Tim's astronaut training:

- Russian language – on the International Space Station astronauts speak English and Russian.

- Spaceflight science and engineering – astronauts have to be able to fix the Space Station and understand how spacecraft fly.

- Rescue and survival skills – these skills are needed in case an astronaut lands in the sea, a desert or a forest when they return to Earth from the Space Station.

- Basic medical training – you can't pop to the dentist or hospital if you are in space!

- **Weightlessness** training – when astronauts are in space, they float. They need to learn how to move around while floating.

Weightlessness training is very important. Floating might sound fun, but in space it can make some people feel sick. Trainee astronauts take special plane flights that mimic weightlessness to help them get used to how it feels.

Astronauts also prepare for weightlessness by doing lots of training underwater in their spacesuits. This is because floating in water is similar to floating in space. As part of Tim's training, he spent a week in an underwater cave. He also lived for 12 days underwater, learning how to do scientific experiments while floating.

After all this training, it was finally time to blast off! On 15th December 2015, Tim launched into space. He spent six months at the Space Station. In that time, he took part in over 250 scientific experiments.

Many experiments are done on the Space Station. Some experiments try to answer big questions like, "What is the universe made of?" Other experiments are about living in space. For example, astronauts are trying to grow their own food in the Space Station.

One of Tim's most memorable experiences in space was a four-hour spacewalk. A spacewalk is when astronauts work outside of a spacecraft.

Tim went on his spacewalk to repair a damaged solar panel on the Space Station. Energy produced by the solar panel wasn't reaching the rest of the Space Station. The repair kept the station's power supply working properly.

Tim wore a spacesuit on his spacewalk to keep himself safe. A spacesuit has a supply of oxygen so the astronaut can breathe. It also contains some drinking water. It stops the astronaut getting too hot or too cold. Without a spacesuit, it is impossible to survive outside a spacecraft.

Tim wanted to inspire children to find out more about science and space. From space, Tim took amazing photos of our planet. He shared these with children back down on Earth.

More than 1.6 million children from across Europe took part in 30 science projects with Tim. In one project, schools received seeds that had been in space. They measured the plants that grew from the seeds. They then compared these plants with plants grown from seeds that had not been in space. The results showed that the space seeds grew slightly less well than the seeds that had stayed on Earth.

Tim's time at the Space Station was very busy, but he made time for one further challenge – running a **marathon** in space! He ran it to raise money for a charity that works with young people. The Space Station is quite small, so he had to run on a **treadmill**. The marathon took him 3 hours, 35 minutes and 21 seconds!

So how did Tim run on a treadmill without floating away? He wore a harness a bit like a backpack that he hooked onto stretchy straps on the treadmill. This kept Tim's feet in contact with the treadmill.

Tim is now back on Earth again, but he hopes to return to the Space Station one day. Tim continues to encourage children and young people to be interested in space exploration. After all, children are the explorers of the future.

Where do you think people will explore next? It could be Mars, the moons of Neptune, or even another universe!

Bonus

The International Space Station

It is the biggest spacecraft ever flown in space. It is almost the size of a football pitch.

1 **Modules**
This is where the astronauts live and work.

2 **Solar panels**
These turn sunlight into electricity.

3 **Radiators**
These send unwanted heat into space.

4 **Spacecraft**
Astronauts use this to travel to and from the space station.

5 **Robotic arm**
This moves **supplies** for the space station.

Glossary

circumnavigate sail all the way around

climate change long-term changes in temperature and rainfall

cocoon the covering made by some insects to protect themselves as they develop into adults

currents movements of water in the sea

glaciers slowly-moving rivers of ice

humid warm and damp

igloo an Inuit round house built of blocks of hard snow

Inuit people living in northern Canada and Greenland

marathon a long-distance running race, about 26.2 miles (42 km) long

naturalist an expert in plants, animals and insects

navigating to make sure that a thing or person is going in the right direction

network a group of things that are connected to each other, for example passageways or caves

traded bought, sold or swapped things

treadmill an exercise machine you can run on

vines climbing plants, such as grape plants

weightlessness the feeling of almost no weight, which can feel like floating

About the author

Why did you want to write this book?
I learnt about Maria Sibylla Merian's voyage after seeing her paintings in a museum in the Netherlands. I thought her story was fascinating. It made me ask myself: Which other amazing explorers have I never heard of?

Hawys Morgan

Do you have a favourite voyage or person in this book?
I admire them all! Each explorer overcomes different problems in order to make their voyage a success. I have a lot of respect for their determination. I think it takes a very special type of person to face these challenges.

Where and when do you like to write?
I usually write at home. I never write when I'm travelling. I prefer to concentrate on taking in the new sights, sounds and smells of the place I'm visiting. These experiences all get stored somewhere in my memory and will pop out on the page at some later date.

Do you write better in the morning?
My favourite time to write is in the morning. As soon as my children have gone to school, I make myself a big mug of tea and then I start typing.

How do you go about writing a book like this?
I start by asking myself questions, such as, "Who was the first person to reach the North Pole?" Then I do a lot of research! I like to know the backstories of the people I write about. This helps me understand how they can keep going even when times are tough. I also look at photos of the different places these explorers visited. It's important for me to get a real feel for what their journeys might have been like.

Would you like to go on any of the voyages in this book?
I would like to follow Jeanne Baret's voyage around the world. She saw so many different landscapes, plants and animals during her long journey. I think Jill Heinerth is very brave, but I don't fancy cave diving. I think I would find it too scary!

What do you hope readers will get out of the book?
I hope it will make readers believe that anyone can be an explorer. Maybe it will inspire some readers to go on their own epic voyage?

What's the best voyage you've ever been on?
When I was a teenager, I was lucky to go on a trip to South Africa with my parents. Seeing animals like elephants, zebras and giraffes in the wild was an incredible experience that I will never forget.

Book chat

What have you learned from reading this book?

Had you heard of any of these people before reading the book?

Do you have a favourite voyage or person?

Would you like to go on any of the voyages in this book?

Which voyage do you think was the most interesting?

If you could ask any of the people in this book a question, who would you choose and what would you ask?

Who would you recommend this book to and why?

What fact from the book did you find surprising or interesting?

Do you think this book would make a good film? Why or why not?

Who would you recommend this book to and why?

Have you heard of any other epic voyages?

How would you sum up this book in one sentence?

If you could ask the author any question, what would you ask?

Which voyage or voyager would you like to learn more about?

What's the best journey you've ever been on?

Book challenge:
Draw a route for your very own epic voyage.

Published by Collins
An imprint of HarperCollins*Publishers*

The News Building
1 London Bridge Street
London SE1 9GF
UK

Macken House
39/40 Mayor Street Upper
Dublin 1
D01 C9W8
Ireland

© HarperCollins*Publishers* Limited 2024

10 9 8 7 6 5 4 3

ISBN 978-0-00-868120-3

All rights reserved. No part of this publication may be reproduced, stored in a retrieval system, or transmitted in any form by any means, electronic, mechanical, photocopying, recording or otherwise, without the prior written permission of the Publisher or a licence permitting restricted copying in the United Kingdom issued by the Copyright Licensing Agency Ltd, 5th Floor, Shackleton House, 4 Battle Bridge Lane, London SE1 2HX.

Without limiting the exclusive rights of any author, contributor or the publisher, any unauthorised use of this publication to train generative artificial intelligence (AI) technologies is expressly prohibited. HarperCollins also exercise their rights under Article 4(3) of the Digital Single Market Directive 2019/790 and expressly reserve this publication from the text and data mining exception.

British Library Cataloguing-in-Publication Data
A catalogue record for this publication is available from the British Library.

Download the teaching notes and word cards to accompany this book at:
http://littlewandle.org.uk/signupfluency/

Get the latest Collins Big Cat news at
collins.co.uk/collinsbigcat

Author: Hawys Morgan
Illustrators: Alisha Monnin (Astound Illustration Agency) and Roger Stewart (Beehive Illustration)
Publisher: Laura White
Product manager: Caroline Green
Series editor: Charlotte Raby
Development editor: Catherine Baker
Commissioning editor: Suzannah Ditchburn
Project manager: Emily Hooton
Copyeditor: Sally Byford
Permissions researcher: Rachel Thorne
Proofreader: Emily Hooton
Cover designer: Sarah Finan
Typesetter: 2Hoots Publishing Services Ltd
Production controller: Katharine Willard
Printed in the UK.

	MIX
FSC www.fsc.org	Paper | Supporting responsible forestry FSC™ C007454

This book contains FSC™ certified paper and other controlled sources to ensure responsible forest management.

For more information visit: www.harpercollins.co.uk/green

Made with responsibly sourced paper and vegetable ink

Scan to see how we are reducing our environmental impact.

Acknowledgements
The publishers gratefully acknowledge the permission granted to reproduce the copyright material in this book. Every effort has been made to trace copyright holders and to obtain their permission for the use of copyright material. The publishers will gladly receive any information enabling them to rectify any error or omission at the first opportunity.

With thanks to Tim Peake

With thanks to Jill Heinerth, *Into The Planet*.

Front cover courtesy of Jill Heinerth/*Into The Planet*, p13t Eric Isselee/Shutterstock, p13b All Canada Photos/Alamy, p13 (background) Lukasz Szwaj/Shutterstock, p18 incamerastock/Alamy, p19 hxdbzxy/Shutterstock, p21 Florilegius/Alamy, p22 Kim Howell/Shutterstock, p28 Album/Alamy, p29 reptiles4all/Shutterstock, p29t alslutsky/Shutterstock, p29c Joel Sartore/Photo Ark/Nature Picture Library, p29b reptiles4all/Shutterstock, pp30–31 Protasov AN/Shutterstock, p31bl Eric Isselee/Shutterstock, p46 Science History Images/Alamy, p56 Tango Images/Alamy, p57 Associated Press/Alamy, pp63–67 & 69 Courtesy of Jill Heinerth, p68 imageBROKER.com/Shutterstock, p72 ESA, p73 NASA, p74 Sasa Kadrijevic/Alamy, p75 ESA, p76 ESA, p77 NASA, p78 ESA, p79 ESA, p80 Associated Press/Alamy, p81 ESA, pp82–83 NG Images/Alamy, back cover tr Sepia Times/Universal Images Group/Getty Images, bl Geopix/Alamy, br Archive Photos/Stringer/Getty Images.